EMMANUEL JOSEPH

Strategic Justice, Military and ICC's Dance with Geopolitics

Copyright © 2025 by Emmanuel Joseph

All rights reserved. No part of this publication may be reproduced, stored or transmitted in any form or by any means, electronic, mechanical, photocopying, recording, scanning, or otherwise without written permission from the publisher. It is illegal to copy this book, post it to a website, or distribute it by any other means without permission.

First edition

This book was professionally typeset on Reedsy.
Find out more at reedsy.com

Contents

1 Chapter 1: The Genesis of the International Criminal Court... 1
2 Chapter 2: Military Influence in Global Governance 3
3 Chapter 3: The ICC's Jurisdiction and Sovereignty Dilemma 5
4 Chapter 4: The Influence of Geopolitical Interests 7
5 Chapter 5: The Role of the Military in ICC Prosecutions... 9
6 Chapter 6: The Impact of ICC Prosecutions on Geopolitical... 11
7 Chapter 7: The Challenges of Enforcing ICC Judgments 13
8 Chapter 8: The ICC's Impact on Domestic Legal Systems 15
9 Chapter 9: The Role of Civil Society in Supporting the ICC 17
10 Chapter 10: The Future of the ICC in a Changing Geopolitical... 19
11 Chapter 11: Lessons Learned from ICC's Past Experiences 21
12 Chapter 12: The Vision for a Just and Equitable Future 23

1

Chapter 1: The Genesis of the International Criminal Court (ICC)

The inception of the International Criminal Court (ICC) in 2002 was a landmark event in the history of international justice. Born out of the Rome Statute of 1998, the ICC sought to address the world's most heinous crimes: genocide, war crimes, and crimes against humanity. It aimed to provide a mechanism for holding individuals accountable, transcending the limitations of national jurisdictions. The establishment of the ICC was a response to the atrocities that had marred the 20th century, particularly the Rwandan Genocide and the Balkan Wars.

The ICC was intended to operate independently of any single nation or political influence, striving to uphold justice impartially. This independence was enshrined in its foundational documents, emphasizing its role as a court of last resort. It was designed to step in only when national judicial systems were unwilling or unable to prosecute offenders. The court's establishment was hailed as a triumph for human rights advocates who had long sought a permanent international tribunal.

However, the ICC's journey has been fraught with challenges from the outset. Critics argued that it lacked the necessary enforcement mechanisms to execute its mandate effectively. The court's reliance on member states for cooperation, such as arresting suspects and providing evidence, was seen as a significant weakness. Furthermore, questions about the court's jurisdiction and its ability to prosecute sitting heads of state added to the controversy.

Despite these challenges, the ICC began its operations with a sense of mission and urgency. Early cases focused on warlords and political leaders from conflict zones, such as the Democratic Republic of Congo and Sudan. The court's first prosecutor, Luis Moreno-Ocampo, became a prominent figure, symbolizing the ICC's commitment to justice. Nonetheless, the road ahead was uncertain, with geopolitical dynamics playing a crucial role in shaping the court's effectiveness.

The ICC's creation was a bold experiment in international justice, reflecting the world's desire for accountability and the rule of law. Yet, its dependence on political will and state cooperation underscored the complex interplay between justice and geopolitics. As the ICC embarked on its mission, it would soon find itself entangled in the intricate web of global power dynamics.

2

Chapter 2: Military Influence in Global Governance

The role of the military in global governance has always been a double-edged sword. On one hand, military power is essential for maintaining peace and security; on the other, it can be a tool for oppression and conflict. Throughout history, the military has played a pivotal role in shaping the world order, often dictating the terms of peace and justice. This influence extends to the realm of international justice, where military considerations often intersect with legal and moral imperatives.

Military interventions in conflict zones can create conditions for accountability, but they can also complicate the pursuit of justice. The use of force to stop atrocities, as seen in interventions like NATO's in Kosovo or the coalition forces in Iraq, raises questions about the legitimacy and consequences of such actions. These interventions are often justified on humanitarian grounds, but they inevitably lead to debates about sovereignty and the rule of law.

The military's involvement in international justice is not limited to direct interventions. Military leaders and personnel can be both perpetrators and protectors of human rights. The prosecution of military officials for war crimes, such as those seen in the trials of former Yugoslav generals, highlights the complex relationship between the armed forces and the justice system. These cases underscore the need for accountability while acknowledging the unique challenges posed by military hierarchies and command structures.

Moreover, the military's strategic interests often influence decisions about whether and how to pursue justice. Governments may be reluctant to cooperate with international courts if it jeopardizes their military alliances or strategic objectives. This dynamic can result in selective justice, where certain crimes are prosecuted while others are overlooked. The tension between military strategy and legal accountability is a persistent theme in the discourse on international justice.

The interplay between the military and global governance is a microcosm of the broader struggle to balance power and principle. As the ICC navigates this landscape, it must contend with the realities of military influence and the need for cooperation from states with powerful armed forces. This intricate dance between justice and geopolitics defines the court's operational context and challenges its ability to deliver impartial justice.

3

Chapter 3: The ICC's Jurisdiction and Sovereignty Dilemma

The issue of jurisdiction is central to the ICC's mandate, yet it remains one of the most contentious aspects of its operations. The court's jurisdiction is limited to crimes committed on the territory of member states or by their nationals. This constraint poses significant challenges, particularly when dealing with non-member states or situations where the crimes span multiple jurisdictions. The ICC's ability to exercise its mandate is often hindered by political and legal complexities surrounding sovereignty.

Sovereignty, the principle that states have supreme authority within their territories, is a cornerstone of international law. However, this principle can clash with the ICC's mission to prosecute international crimes. When a state is unwilling or unable to prosecute, the ICC can step in, but this intervention is often perceived as an infringement on sovereignty. The tension between state sovereignty and international justice is a recurring theme in the court's operations.

The ICC's interventions in non-member states, such as its investigations in Afghanistan and Myanmar, have sparked significant controversy. These interventions are based on UN Security Council referrals or the court's proprio motu powers, but they are often met with resistance from the states involved. Accusations of political bias and neo-colonialism have been leveled against the ICC, particularly by countries in the Global South. These criticisms highlight the geopolitical dimensions of the court's work.

Moreover, the ICC's reliance on state cooperation for enforcement further complicates its jurisdictional challenges. Arrest warrants issued by the court often go unexecuted, as states may be unwilling or unable to apprehend suspects. The case of Sudanese President Omar al-Bashir, who evaded arrest despite ICC warrants, exemplifies the limitations of the court's jurisdictional reach. The reliance on political will and state compliance underscores the fragile nature of the ICC's authority.

The jurisdictional and sovereignty dilemma is a fundamental challenge that the ICC must navigate. Balancing respect for state sovereignty with the imperative of international justice requires a nuanced approach. The court's efforts to address this challenge will shape its future trajectory and its ability to fulfill its mandate of accountability and justice.

4

Chapter 4: The Influence of Geopolitical Interests

Geopolitical interests play a pivotal role in shaping the landscape of international justice. The ICC, as an institution operating within the global political arena, is inevitably influenced by the strategic priorities and alliances of powerful states. This influence can manifest in various ways, from the selection of cases to the level of cooperation extended by states. The interplay between justice and geopolitics is a defining feature of the ICC's work.

The selective nature of ICC prosecutions has been a point of contention, with critics arguing that the court disproportionately targets African leaders while overlooking crimes committed by powerful states. This perception is fueled by the geopolitical realities of international justice, where the interests of influential states can shape the court's agenda. The reliance on state cooperation for enforcement and the need for political support at the UN Security Council further exacerbate these dynamics.

The ICC's dependence on funding from member states also introduces geopolitical considerations. Financial contributions from powerful states can influence the court's priorities and operations. The withdrawal of support, as seen with the US's decision to impose sanctions on ICC officials investigating American personnel, underscores the vulnerability of the court to geopolitical pressures. These financial and political dependencies highlight the challenges of maintaining the ICC's independence and impartiality.

The role of the UN Security Council in referring cases to the ICC also underscores the geopolitical dimensions of international justice. The council's composition, with its permanent members wielding veto power, means that political considerations often shape decisions about which situations are referred to the court. This dynamic can result in the ICC being used as a tool of political leverage, rather than an impartial instrument of justice.

The influence of geopolitical interests on the ICC is a reflection of the broader challenges faced by international institutions in navigating the complexities of global power dynamics. The court's ability to uphold its mandate of impartial justice is contingent on its capacity to manage these influences while maintaining its credibility. The dance between justice and geopolitics is a delicate one, requiring constant vigilance and adaptability.

5

Chapter 5: The Role of the Military in ICC Prosecutions (continued)

The reluctance of military authorities to cooperate with the ICC can stem from various factors, including concerns about national security, political stability, and the potential impact on military morale. This reluctance can hinder the ICC's ability to gather evidence and prosecute cases effectively. The court must navigate these challenges by building trust and fostering cooperation with military and civilian authorities.

The ICC has also faced challenges in prosecuting military personnel due to issues of command responsibility. Holding senior military leaders accountable for the actions of their subordinates requires proving that they had effective control over their forces and failed to prevent or punish crimes. This legal standard can be difficult to meet, particularly in complex conflict situations where command structures may be opaque or fragmented.

Despite these challenges, the ICC's efforts to prosecute military personnel for war crimes underscore the importance of accountability in the armed forces. The court's work highlights the need for rigorous legal standards and robust mechanisms for investigating and prosecuting crimes committed by military personnel. By holding military leaders accountable, the ICC aims to deter future atrocities and promote adherence to international humanitarian law.

The military's role in ICC prosecutions also extends to the protection of witnesses and victims. Ensuring the safety of those who testify before the court is crucial for the integrity of the judicial process. Military forces can play a vital role in providing security and support for witnesses, particularly in conflict zones where the threat of retaliation is high. The ICC's witness protection program relies on cooperation with military and civilian authorities to safeguard the rights and wellbeing of witnesses.

In conclusion, the role of the military in ICC prosecutions is complex and multifaceted. The court's ability to hold military personnel accountable for war crimes depends on effective cooperation with military and civilian authorities, robust legal standards, and a commitment to justice. The ICC's work in this area underscores the broader challenges of balancing security, accountability, and the rule of law in the pursuit of international justice.

6

Chapter 6: The Impact of ICC Prosecutions on Geopolitical Dynamics

The ICC's prosecutions have a profound impact on geopolitical dynamics, influencing the behavior of states and shaping international relations. The court's interventions can alter the strategic calculus of political and military leaders, prompting changes in policy and behavior. The ICC's role as a mechanism of accountability can serve as a deterrent to future crimes, but it can also provoke resistance and backlash from those who feel threatened by its mandate.

One of the most significant impacts of ICC prosecutions is the potential to influence peace processes and conflict resolution efforts. The court's interventions can complicate negotiations and make it difficult to reach political settlements, particularly when key actors are under investigation or facing prosecution. This dynamic can create tensions between the pursuit of justice and the need for peace, leading to debates about the appropriate role of the ICC in conflict situations.

The ICC's interventions can also affect the legitimacy and stability of governments. Prosecutions of political and military leaders can delegitimize regimes accused of committing atrocities, leading to internal and external pressure for change. However, these interventions can also destabilize governments, particularly in fragile states where political power is contested.

The ICC's actions can contribute to political instability, complicating efforts to achieve lasting peace and security.

Furthermore, the ICC's prosecutions can influence international alliances and diplomatic relations. States may adjust their foreign policies in response to the court's actions, either by supporting or opposing its interventions. The ICC's investigations can become a focal point for international diplomacy, with states leveraging their influence to shape the court's agenda. This dynamic underscores the intersection of justice and geopolitics in the ICC's work.

The impact of ICC prosecutions on geopolitical dynamics highlights the complex interplay between justice and international relations. The court's interventions can have far-reaching consequences, shaping the behavior of states and influencing the course of global events. The ICC's efforts to balance its mandate of accountability with the realities of geopolitics will continue to shape its role in the international system.

7

Chapter 7: The Challenges of Enforcing ICC Judgments

Enforcing ICC judgments is one of the most significant challenges facing the court. The ICC lacks its own enforcement mechanisms and relies on member states for the arrest and transfer of suspects, as well as the implementation of its judgments. This reliance on state cooperation creates a significant vulnerability, as the court's ability to execute its mandate depends on the willingness and capacity of states to comply with its orders.

The case of Sudanese President Omar al-Bashir, who evaded arrest despite multiple ICC warrants, exemplifies the difficulties of enforcing the court's judgments. Al-Bashir's ability to travel freely, even to states that are parties to the Rome Statute, highlighted the limitations of the ICC's enforcement capabilities. The court's reliance on political will and state cooperation underscores the challenges of achieving accountability in the face of geopolitical realities.

The ICC has also faced challenges in securing the cooperation of states for the execution of its sentences. The imprisonment of convicted individuals requires the support of states willing to host them, and the court has encountered difficulties in finding states willing to assume this responsibility. The lack of a permanent detention facility further complicates the ICC's ability to enforce its judgments and underscores the need for greater international support.

The ICC's reliance on state cooperation also extends to the protection of victims and witnesses. Ensuring the safety of those who participate in the court's proceedings is crucial for the integrity of the judicial process. However, the court has faced challenges in securing adequate protection for witnesses, particularly in conflict zones where the threat of retaliation is high. The ICC's witness protection program relies on the cooperation of states and international organizations to provide the necessary support.

The challenges of enforcing ICC judgments highlight the broader issues of political will and state cooperation in the pursuit of international justice. The court's ability to achieve its mandate depends on the commitment of the international community to uphold the principles of accountability and the rule of law. Strengthening the mechanisms for enforcing ICC judgments will be crucial for the court's effectiveness and credibility.

8

Chapter 8: The ICC's Impact on Domestic Legal Systems

The ICC's interventions can have a significant impact on domestic legal systems, shaping the development of national accountability mechanisms and influencing the behavior of judicial authorities. The principle of complementarity, which underpins the ICC's mandate, emphasizes the role of national courts in prosecuting international crimes. The ICC's involvement can serve as a catalyst for domestic legal reforms and the strengthening of national judicial systems.

The ICC's interventions have prompted several states to enhance their legal frameworks for addressing international crimes. The incorporation of international standards into domestic law, as seen in countries like Kenya and Colombia, reflects the influence of the ICC's mandate. These reforms can improve the capacity of national courts to prosecute crimes that fall within the ICC's jurisdiction, contributing to the broader goals of accountability and justice.

The ICC's involvement can also incentivize states to take action against perpetrators of international crimes, particularly in situations where the threat of ICC prosecution looms. The court's presence can prompt governments to initiate domestic investigations and prosecutions to demonstrate their commitment to accountability. This dynamic underscores the complementary relationship between the ICC and national legal systems in the pursuit of justice.

However, the ICC's interventions can also create challenges for domestic legal systems. The court's involvement can strain the resources and capacities of national judicial authorities, particularly in conflict-affected states. The demands of cooperating with the ICC, including the provision of evidence and the protection of witnesses, can place significant burdens on domestic institutions. Balancing the requirements of international justice with the needs of national legal systems is a complex and ongoing challenge.

The impact of the ICC on domestic legal systems highlights the interconnectedness of international and national accountability mechanisms. The court's efforts to promote justice at the international level can have far-reaching implications for the development of domestic legal frameworks and the capacity of national courts to address international crimes. Strengthening the relationship between the ICC and domestic legal systems will be crucial for achieving the goals of accountability and justice.

9

Chapter 9: The Role of Civil Society in Supporting the ICC

Civil society organizations play a vital role in supporting the ICC and promoting the goals of international justice. These organizations, including human rights groups, legal advocacy organizations, and grassroots movements, contribute to the ICC's work by providing evidence, advocating for justice, and raising awareness about the court's mandate. The involvement of civil society is crucial for the ICC's effectiveness and legitimacy.

Human rights organizations often play a key role in documenting atrocities and providing evidence to the ICC. These organizations are often on the frontlines of conflict zones, gathering crucial information about crimes and identifying perpetrators. The documentation provided by human rights groups can be instrumental in building cases and securing convictions. The collaboration between civil society and the ICC underscores the importance of grassroots efforts in the pursuit of justice.

Legal advocacy organizations also contribute to the ICC's work by providing expertise and supporting legal reforms. These organizations often work to strengthen the legal frameworks for prosecuting international crimes and promote the principles of international justice. By advocating for the incorporation of international standards into domestic law, legal advocacy groups help create an environment conducive to accountability and justice.

Grassroots movements and victim advocacy organizations play a crucial role in raising awareness about the ICC and mobilizing support for its mandate. These organizations often represent the voices of victims and survivors, advocating for justice and reparations. The involvement of grassroots movements can amplify the demands for accountability and contribute to the ICC's efforts to address the needs of affected communities.

The role of civil society in supporting the ICC highlights the importance of a multi-faceted approach to international justice. The collaboration between civil society organizations and the ICC strengthens the court's ability to fulfill its mandate and promotes a more inclusive and participatory approach to justice. Recognizing and supporting the contributions of civil society will be crucial for the ICC's continued effectiveness and legitimacy.

10

Chapter 10: The Future of the ICC in a Changing Geopolitical Landscape

The future of the ICC is shaped by the evolving geopolitical landscape and the challenges of addressing international crimes in a complex and interconnected world. The court's ability to fulfill its mandate depends on its capacity to adapt to changing global dynamics and the willingness of the international community to support its mission. As the ICC navigates these challenges, several key trends and developments will influence its trajectory.

One significant trend is the rise of multipolarity in the international system. The emergence of new global powers and the shifting balance of power create a more complex and competitive geopolitical environment. This multipolarity can impact the ICC's operations, as states may use the court as a tool of political leverage or resist its interventions to protect their strategic interests. The ICC will need to navigate these dynamics while maintaining its commitment to impartial justice.

Another important development is the increasing emphasis on regional justice mechanisms. Regional courts and tribunals, such as the African Court on Human and Peoples' Rights, are playing a more prominent role in addressing international crimes. These regional mechanisms can complement the ICC's work by providing additional avenues for accountability and justice.

The ICC's relationship with regional courts and the broader international justice system will be crucial for its future effectiveness.

The ICC must also contend with the challenges posed by emerging technologies and new forms of conflict. The use of cyber warfare, autonomous weapons, and other advanced technologies in conflicts presents new legal and ethical questions for the court. The ICC will need to adapt its legal frameworks and investigative methods to address these emerging threats and ensure accountability in the digital age. This adaptation will require collaboration with experts in technology, law, and human rights.

The role of civil society and grassroots movements will continue to be essential for the ICC's success. These organizations play a crucial role in documenting crimes, advocating for justice, and supporting victims. The ICC's ability to engage with and support civil society will be vital for its legitimacy and effectiveness. Strengthening partnerships with civil society organizations and incorporating their perspectives into the court's work will enhance its ability to address the needs of affected communities.

In conclusion, the future of the ICC is shaped by a dynamic and evolving geopolitical landscape. The court's ability to fulfill its mandate depends on its capacity to adapt to changing global dynamics, engage with regional and civil society partners, and address emerging challenges. By navigating these complexities, the ICC can continue to play a vital role in promoting accountability and justice in the international system.

11

Chapter 11: Lessons Learned from ICC's Past Experiences

The experiences of the ICC over the past two decades provide valuable lessons for the future of international justice. The court's successes and challenges offer insights into the complexities of prosecuting international crimes and the importance of balancing legal, political, and ethical considerations. Reflecting on these lessons can inform the ICC's future strategies and enhance its ability to fulfill its mandate.

One key lesson is the importance of state cooperation for the effectiveness of the ICC. The court's reliance on member states for enforcement, evidence, and witness protection underscores the need for strong partnerships and political support. The challenges faced in securing the arrest and transfer of suspects, as seen in the case of Omar al-Bashir, highlight the limitations of the ICC's enforcement capabilities. Building stronger mechanisms for state cooperation and accountability will be crucial for the court's success.

Another lesson is the need for greater inclusivity and diversity in the ICC's operations. The perception of bias and selective justice, particularly in the targeting of African leaders, has undermined the court's legitimacy in some quarters. Enhancing the representation of diverse voices and perspectives within the ICC, including those from the Global South, can strengthen its credibility and address concerns of bias. Promoting inclusivity and fairness in the court's work is essential for its legitimacy and effectiveness.

The ICC's experiences also highlight the importance of balancing justice and peace in conflict situations. The court's interventions can impact peace processes and political settlements, creating tensions between the pursuit of justice and the need for stability. The ICC must navigate these dynamics carefully, ensuring that its actions contribute to sustainable peace and justice. Engaging with conflict resolution experts and stakeholders can help the court balance these imperatives.

The role of civil society and grassroots movements in supporting the ICC is another critical lesson. These organizations play a vital role in documenting crimes, advocating for justice, and raising awareness about the court's mandate. The collaboration between civil society and the ICC strengthens the court's ability to fulfill its mission and promotes a more inclusive approach to justice. Recognizing and supporting the contributions of civil society will be crucial for the ICC's future effectiveness.

In conclusion, the lessons learned from the ICC's past experiences provide valuable insights for the future of international justice. Building stronger state cooperation, promoting inclusivity, balancing justice and peace, and engaging with civil society are essential strategies for the court's success. By reflecting on these lessons, the ICC can enhance its ability to promote accountability and justice in the international system.

12

Chapter 12: The Vision for a Just and Equitable Future

The vision for a just and equitable future is one where the principles of accountability, fairness, and the rule of law are upheld at all levels of society. The ICC plays a crucial role in this vision by providing a mechanism for addressing the world's most serious crimes and promoting justice on a global scale. As the court continues its mission, it must strive to embody these principles and contribute to a more just and equitable world.

Achieving this vision requires a commitment to the core values of impartiality and independence. The ICC must uphold these values in its operations, ensuring that its interventions are guided by the pursuit of justice rather than political considerations. Maintaining the court's independence from external influences and upholding the highest standards of fairness and integrity are essential for its legitimacy and effectiveness.

The vision for a just and equitable future also requires a focus on inclusivity and representation. The ICC must strive to represent diverse voices and perspectives, particularly those from marginalized and affected communities. Enhancing the participation of victims, survivors, and civil society in the court's work can promote a more inclusive approach to justice and address concerns of bias. Inclusivity is a cornerstone of a just and equitable international justice system.

Promoting accountability and deterrence is another key aspect of this vision. The ICC's mandate to prosecute international crimes serves as a deterrent to future atrocities and reinforces the principle that no one is above the law. By holding perpetrators accountable, the court contributes to a culture of accountability and strengthens the rule of law. The ICC's efforts to promote justice and accountability are essential for a more just and equitable world.

Finally, the vision for a just and equitable future requires a commitment to cooperation and collaboration. The ICC must work in partnership with states, international organizations, civil society, and other stakeholders to achieve its mission. Strengthening these partnerships and fostering a collaborative approach to justice can enhance the court's effectiveness and contribute to the broader goals of peace and security.

In conclusion, the vision for a just and equitable future is one where accountability, fairness, and the rule of law are upheld on a global scale. The ICC's role in this vision is crucial, and its efforts to promote justice and accountability are essential for a more just and equitable world. By upholding its core values, promoting inclusivity, and fostering cooperation, the ICC can contribute to a brighter future for all.

Strategic Justice: Military and ICC's Dance with Geopolitics

In "Strategic Justice: Military and ICC's Dance with Geopolitics," dive into the intricate and often tumultuous relationship between the military, international justice, and the geopolitical landscape. This book unravels the complex dynamics that shape the International Criminal Court's (ICC) quest for accountability while navigating the power plays of global politics.

The journey begins with the genesis of the ICC, a beacon of hope for addressing the world's gravest crimes. Through its establishment, the book explores the court's mission, challenges, and the critical role it plays in holding individuals accountable for genocide, war crimes, and crimes against humanity. As the narrative unfolds, readers gain insights into the delicate balance the ICC must strike between justice and state sovereignty.

The book delves into the military's profound influence on global governance, highlighting how military interventions, both as perpetrators and protectors, intersect with the realm of international justice. It examines the

CHAPTER 12: THE VISION FOR A JUST AND EQUITABLE FUTURE

thorny issues of military prosecutions, command responsibility, and the often fraught cooperation between military forces and the ICC.

Geopolitical interests take center stage as the book reveals how powerful states shape the ICC's agenda. It scrutinizes the selective nature of prosecutions, the court's dependence on member states for enforcement, and the intricate dance between the ICC and the United Nations Security Council. These dynamics underscore the constant interplay between justice and global power.

As the narrative progresses, readers are taken through the ICC's impact on domestic legal systems, the vital role of civil society, and the lessons learned from the court's past experiences. The book offers a thoughtful reflection on the future of the ICC in an ever-changing geopolitical landscape, emphasizing the need for adaptability, cooperation, and a commitment to inclusivity and fairness.

"Strategic Justice: Military and ICC's Dance with Geopolitics" is an enlightening exploration of the ICC's efforts to promote accountability and justice. It challenges readers to consider the complex realities of international justice and the enduring quest for a just and equitable world.

www.ingramcontent.com/pod-product-compliance
Lightning Source LLC
LaVergne TN
LVHW020743090526
838202LV00057BA/6216